RUNNING
TO THE GRAVE

RUNNING
TO THE GRAVE

BASED ON A TRUE STORY

by CHERRYL FUGATE

Charleston, SC
www.PalmettoPublishing.com

Running to the Grave

First Edition

Paperback ISBN: 979-8-88590-325-7

CHAPTER 1

In the early years of his life, Desmond Burns grew up in a small village in Greenwood, Guyana, where everyone knew each other and people looked out for one another. Desmond was very well mannered and always neatly dressed, even though his clothes were mostly rags. He would wear them with pride and would always coordinate the colors of his clothes so they would look good on him. Desmond was born to his parents John and Ethel Burns: his mother was a stay-at-home mom, and his dad was a plantation farmer. His father was a nonspiritual twenty-four years old and his mother an appealing twenty-two years old when they met. His dad worked the crops so that the family could put food on the table. His father, who was a heavy drinker and hot-tempered man, scared the heck out of him, so Desmond would try not to piss off his father in any way.

Desmond's dad would take him to the plantation so he could learn to work the fields, but Desmond hated to go there with his dad. He thought that he could do better than working on the plantation—whenever Desmond would try to talk to his father about not wanting to work in the fields, he would get lashes across his back because his father thought that Desmond was being disrespectful. His mother used to sit to the side and watch her son get flogged for something he didn't want to do, and when she would intervene, she also got hit by her angry husband. Desmond's mother was a Methodist, and her belief as a follower of God was that he alone was worthy of honor and praise. His mother, who always tried to be a good submissive Christian wife, would try to sit her husband down and explain salvation to him, but he just couldn't get it. Desmond's father was an alcoholic, and his mother was battling the emotional turmoil of their family.

Desmond's father would bring home money when the crops sold. He would give his wife most of the money and keep some for himself. Then he would go to the local bar and have drinks with other plantation workers and pick up local hookers and get drunk. He would come home and try to have sex with his wife. His disgusting smell of liquor and cheap perfume would make her want to puke. And when she refused due to his smell, he would try to force himself on top of her. Desmond would be awakened by the loud noise and would yell from his room, asking his mother if she was okay. But his father would yell back, saying, "Stay in your room, boy!"

But he would go on screaming, "Leave her alone!" and the assaults would stop.

Desmond's father would leave the bedroom, go into the kitchen, fix himself a drink, and then go into the living room and fall asleep on the couch. When it was quiet, Desmond would go into his mother's room and make sure she was okay. His mother would hug him and tell him to go back to bed, saying she would be fine. She'd explain to him, "Your father loves us; he's just going through some things." She would say anything to her son to protect her abusive husband and also let her son think his father did love him.

Desmond knew that was far from the truth. One night, he left his mother's room and went into the kitchen grab a bat, then went back to the living room and stood angrily over his sleeping, drunk father. He wanted to crack open his skull for the way his father treated him and his mother, but at that moment, his mother came out of her room, saw him, and convinced him not to do it. He had to grow up enduring his father's abusive behavior toward him and his mom, and he was traumatized by it.

■ ■ ■

One morning after Mr. Burns left for work, Mrs. Burns went to have her morning shower and noticed there was blood in the bathroom sink. The farmer's wife jumped to the conclusion that it was her husband's blood since Desmond had his own bathroom. After her shower she headed to her closet to get dressed. As she was looking to put on something comfortable, her fingers came across a dress she hadn't worn in a while. It was just hanging there on its old plastic hanger; she wanted to put it on, but it was too fancy to wear around the house.

"Oh, how I love this dress!" she exclaimed. "It makes me feel elegant and slender whenever I wear it. I'd die a slow death if I wore it and it got soiled."

She hung it back in the closet and found something more suitable.

Later in the evening, when Mr. Burns came home from work, his wife told him about the blood in the sink. He then told her it was his blood, and he didn't want to alarm her. She told him he needed to see a doctor to find out what was going on. He took his wife's advice, and she accompanied her husband to the hospital. He was sixty-five years old then and was diagnosed with liver disease due to thirty years of alcoholism. Desmond felt resentment toward his ailing and extremely abusive father, who had brought him years of panic and resentment.

■ ■ ■

As time went by, Desmond's dad became sicker and was unable to work. To keep food on the table, Desmond, who was full of bitterness, had to quit school and went with his mother to work the fields. It was not uncommon for women to work on the plantation. The young boy worked side by side with his mother and told her that for his nineteenth birthday, he wanted to join the army and serve his country. His mother was not too happy about that. She said to him, "It's good you want to serve your country, but you can also die in doing so." But his mind was made up about what he wanted to do.

CHAPTER 2

$\mathcal{I}$t was two weeks shy of Desmond's nineteenth birthday. Mother and son woke up at their usual time to prepare to go into the fields. His mom looked over to her husband's side of the bed and realized he had gone to meet the Lord. She touched his cold body and said a prayer, and she left the room. She went into the kitchen, where Desmond was getting meals ready for them to go to work. His mom told him what had happened. He sank into a chair and said to his mother, "He will not be able to hurt us anymore, Mom." He did not shed a tear for his dad. He was just stone cold; his anger wouldn't let him feel any sympathy for his father. His mother asked him to go pass the word around so that the other neighbors would know to come over and help the Burn's bury their husband and father.

The villagers came together to support the family and laid the dead man to rest. As life continued for the Burns family, Desmond started trying to fill the empty space his dad had left. Feeling like the man of the house, he walked over to his dad's favorite rugged old chair and perched on it. He got into a relaxed position and closed his eyes and eventually dozed off into a deep sleep.

His mom made a plate of beans and rice and brought it to the living room to offer it to him, but she saw that he was fast asleep. She noticed him making faces and frightening sounds. She was scared, so she began to tap him, waking him gently. He opened his eyes in fright. His mom said to him, "Son, I think you were having a bad dream."

He said to her, "It was more like a nightmare." He sat up from his position in the chair, and, in a loud voice, he told his mom about the dream. "I saw Pops chasing me through the fields with the bat. I was about to hit him over the head when he was asleep, and he said to me that I would never take his place, that I was not man enough and I was too weak." Desmond asked his mother, "Am I too weak to be a real man?"

His mom responded, "A real man knows how to love and cherish his family, but remember, my son, it was only a dream." Mrs. Burns was still trying to defend her dead husband.

He said to his mother, "When I get married, I will love my family, and I will not let any harm come to them."

His mother, grabbing and hugging him, responded by saying, "You are such a good young man, my son, and I am so proud of you."

"I love you too, Mom," he responded.

CHAPTER 3

The next day, early in the morning before the rooster started crowing to awaken everyone with his cockish noise like an alarm clock, Desmond was already preparing breakfast for himself and his mother to eat before they went into the fields. He cooked plantains and eggs; a healthy breakfast was needed for the kind of work they had to do. Across the hallway, he could hear his mother's footsteps and her softly singing her favorite hymn: "God give me the strength to face another day."

They left their home to prepare for their journey to the plantation. The ground was so dry that, as they walked, you could see the trail of dust they created. It looked like a herd of elephants had just gone by. The rain had not fallen in Greenwood for about a month, so the land was parched. The thirsty soil was eager for a gust of wind to deliver the smell of raindrops.

When Desmond and his mom finally arrived at their work area with thick dust on their feet and faces looking like they were caked with powder, small beads of sweat slowly trickled from their foreheads, making them look as though they had a condition.

Desmond and his mother crossed a wooden bridge to get into the fields. Below the bridge was a stream of clean, black water that was rich in minerals. A steep slope gave way to the stream. The sound of the soothing running water was accompanied by chirping crickets. The tall, beautiful trees that grew alongside the edge of the stream provided shelter and kept the water nice and cool. The workers used the stream to freshen themselves after a hard day's work.

The end of the workweek could not come soon enough for Mrs. Burns. She was happy that she would be able to relax her tired feet for two days until Monday, when she would again have to face the hot, scorching sun and the parched, dry earth if no rain fell.

That night it finally rained. The wind howled like a pack of wolves, and the raindrops drummed heavily on the roof. The downpour helped to extinguish fifteen bush fires and raised the river level: the storm was a real soaker. Not enough to be considered a drought buster, but it made a difference. It renewed the soil and cleaned up the dusty village of Greenwood. The vegetable garden looked healthy and began to produce. Mrs. Burns looked out of the window and said to herself, "God, you knew we needed this."

The early morning dawned cloudy and cool. The grass sure looked greener in Greenwood, and the earth was well moistened. Mrs. Burns was quietly listening to her gospel hymns and trying not to awaken her son, who had just turned nineteen years old. She was so happy and thankful to God that he'd blessed her son's life to see another milestone. Desmond the birthday boy awoke from his sleep, and the smell of his mother's sweet, spicy pumpkin pie was delightful. He knew the scent well because it was his favorite. His mother was wearing the long, white cotton overalls that her mother had worn at the meat locker. His mother also always wore her apron when working in the kitchen. She used it to wipe her perspiring brow when she faced the hot brick oven. An apron in his mother's case was no fashion statement; it was her trademark tool while spending a lot of time in her small kitchen preparing food for her family.

Desmond opened his door and stepped into the kitchen, singing, "Happy birthday to me." He took his mother by the hand and danced with her across the kitchen floor, singing his birthday tune. His mother hugged him and wished him well.

The two sat down for breakfast. While they were having their morning meal, he brought up the subject to his mother of joining the military. He had no intention of working the plantation to earn a living. He was more ambitious than that. He planned to leave the countryside of Greenwood for life in the concrete jungle. He asked his mom to come with him to the city, but she explained to him that Greenwood was her home since she'd grown up there and gotten married to his father there. It was the only life she had ever known. But in the same breath, she said to her son, "I knew the day would come when you would want your own way of life and not to walk in our shadows. All I ask of you, my son, is to come home and visit whenever you have the time."

Desmond went over to the neighbor's house to visit. He told them he was leaving and asked them to look out for his mother since she would be home alone. They told him it was sad to see him go, and they wished him the best of luck. He went back home and started packing his bag to leave early the next morning. His mom made all kinds of dishes for his birthday, and she also wanted him to have enough food for his journey.

He awoke at the crack of dawn early the next morning and tiptoed across the hallway so as not to wake his mom, but she was already up since the day of her son's leaving had come—the day for him to start a new life.

CHAPTER 4

He left the rugged and dusty countryside of Greenwood for a new start in the city of bright lights and asphalt pavement. When Desmond arrived, the sun had set over the city, and the bright moon made it glow. It looked very romantic, although it could get loud over the weekend, when there was live entertainment. As he passed through the city of pleasure, it seemed he might have fallen for the city lights. He felt a tiny tremor of excitement as he gazed in awe. He continued his travel toward the military base, which was about an hour outside the city. While traveling, he thought about his mom and how much he missed her. Desmond finally arrived in the town of Maples. He checked himself into the Blue Note Hotel to pass the night away. As he walked through the revolving door, he was immediately struck by the scent of the gardenia flowers that were placed around the hotel lobby. He was greeted with a friendly smile by the hotel receptionist, and the elegant décor of the hotel created a beautiful ambiance. The room was huge and fancy, a far cry from the room he was used to having in his house back in Greenwood. He stripped his clothes off and hopped into the shower. The bathroom mirror steamed up as he refreshed himself with the hot spray. He turned off the water and came out wrapped in a towel from the waist down. His chest was on display and his face still silky wet.

He walked over to the bed, sat down, and looked around, too restless to sleep, but eventually the enormously tall, powerful young man fluffed his pillow, yanked his blanket over his body, closed his eyes, and fell asleep.

He awoke the next morning to the sound of heavy footsteps in the hallway. He got up, walked to the window, open the curtains, and gazed at the sunshine as it streamed through the glass. His hair and dark, toned body sparkled in the sunlight. He looked down at the ground; the morning sun illuminated shapes in the beautiful landscape. It seemed to him there could be nothing more beautiful than the sun, whose warmth made all things grow. He got himself showered and dressed, left the hotel room, and headed down the road to a local diner to have breakfast. Between sips of coffee, he wolfed down the sandwich the waitress had brought him, glancing at the people going in and out. After breakfast, he pushed away his dish, having eaten every bite off his plate.

He walked out the door of the diner into the courtyard. Desmond stood motionless for a moment, looking with his big brown eyes at the most beautiful girl he had ever seen. He stood and whistled softly. His handsome face gazed at her. She walked up to him. He tried to speak, but it took a few moments before the words would come out of his mouth.

She introduced herself: "Hi, my name is Jade. Did you come in here often when it was owned by the Spades?"

"Oh, no, no," he told her honestly. "I just got into town last night and saw this place and decided to come here for breakfast. I am so sorry; I completely forgot my manners. My name is Desmond Burns," he told her, putting his hand out.

She looked down at his hand for a moment as if she was rather uncertain whether to take it, but then she held out her hand to his. Her full lips curved into a shy smile as she stepped forward to meet him, saying, "It is nice to meet you." He asked her if she would like to have dinner sometime. She responded, "We shall see about that."

He told her where he was staying before they said goodbye to each other. Desmond stood there looking at her as she walked away, saying to himself, "I would sure love to see her again. I don't know if my mind is playing tricks on me, but my gut is telling me that this is not the last time I will see her."

Desmond took a taxi back to the hotel; the morning sun was too hot, and he didn't want to be sweaty. He tried to make conversation with the driver so as not to feel bored, saying things like "What is a moral of a taxi driver?" As he entered the hotel and began to walk down the hall to his room, he could hear loud music coming from a room below. He turned up his TV volume to compete with the music. He crawled into the bed with the blanket and the pillow and fell fast asleep. After wakening about an hour later, he walked over to the window and looked out, wondering what he might see that would catch his interest.

Desmond was consumed with thoughts about Jade. Excited and irritated by these thoughts, he wrote to his mother to tell her how much he loved and missed her and all about his exciting journey into the city. In his letter to his mom, he said, "Dear Mom, I am doing okay. It's weird writing to you because it isn't the same as talking with you. I appreciate the way you always supported me in following my dreams and wanted to see me achieve my goals. I love you, Mom. Got to run. Desmond."

CHAPTER 5

*T*he next morning, he woke up, rubbing his eyes with a lead weight inside his chest, knowing that he was leaving for the army base to be accepted into the military. The sun was up, and the air was warm and particularly pleasant, with the invigorating freshness of morning frost still in the air. He took his morning shower, got dressed, and packed his bags. He headed down to the local diner for breakfast and chose fish fingers, toast, eggs, and bacon. He sat down at table six, a front-row seat to the entrance of the diner, and sipped his coffee, hoping he could see Jade one more time before he left for the base. But he just sat there musing, staring at the lamp flame on the table. He left the diner in some disappointment and began walking down to the bus stop. He could see people's spit glimmer as it flew out of their mouths. In his opinion, regardless of gender, it was improper etiquette to do such disgusting things.

Desmond arrived at the scruffy little bus station. He bought his ticket and boarded the vehicle. It was hot on the bus since there was no air-conditioning. As he sat waiting for the driver to get a move on, sweat ran in rivulets down his back, and his hands were sticky. A pleasant rendering of a classic song was playing. His destination was far away, but he arrived safely despite the heat on the bus.

The army was unprepared for the stampede of young men wanting to fight for the country. The men traded their civilian clothing for military uniforms and took a series of medical and fitness tests before being accepted as soldiers. After all his training was conducted, Desmond became a young recruit entering the army, and then became a soldier after passing all the physicals required by the army. He was very excited and overcome with uncontrolled emotions about the new beginning of his life.

Some of the new recruits were moved to different divisions. Desmond, in a group of twelve, was escorted by military personnel to different barracks. They all got settled and cleaned up, then went to the mess hall for dinner, as they'd been told to do. They were welcomed by top army officials, who introduced themselves. While the officials were getting acquainted with the young men and making them feel comfortable, Desmond began engaging in conversation with some of the superiors. He wanted to make sure he stood out from the other young recruits. While the sergeant spoke about a variety of things, the young soldiers seemed to hang on his every word.

After the evening came to an end, they were sent back to their rooms. Desmond took a shower and set the glowing digits of the alarm clock. He nestled down into the bed and fell asleep. He was awakened by a loud banging on his door. A man with a deep, heavy voice said, "It's time to rise and shine, soldiers." The heavy boots outside his door sounded like a herd of cattle on a stampede at a cattle ranch. He got up, put his gear on, and went out to join the others for physical training. They were given a vigorous high-intensity workout. Some of the soldiers experienced nausea and dizziness. Some of them had to sit the training out. Desmond, a very athletic young man with good body structure and posture, was very happy about the training. He felt like he'd won the Olympics.

As time went by, he made a name for himself in the army. He was very much liked and respected by most of his superior officers. Most of them viewed him as a person who could go very far in the military. Desmond had been in the army for about six months when he was called to the sergeant's office, only to receive the tragic news that his mom had died from a heart attack. He sank into the chair in front of the officer's desk and began sobbing as if his heart had broken. The officer walked over to the young man, placed his hand on his shoulder, and said, "I cannot tell you how sorry I am to hear of your mom's passing. I hope that you will find the inner strength to gather your thoughts in this sad and difficult time."

Desmond was allowed emergency leave to travel home; he was preparing for the most intense emotional experience of his life—his mother's funeral. He remembered that, throughout his years growing up, his mother had always reminded him that there was nothing he couldn't do if he decided to dream big and that he was more than circumstances and labels. Desmond thought, "My mom also taught me how to be compassionate and love with humility. Even though while growing up, we had very little, I remember people would always think we had a lot because my mom would give away the last she had to a stranger and would always say that God would bless us with more. I used to love to listen to my mom reading me stories. I would sit so close to her. It was the best time when my mother would read to me."

As he was nearing his house, he noticed lots of lights and people moving back and forth. There was a small gathering of men and women at one side of the house singing hymns of praise. He was greeted with a warm, hospitable welcome, with lots of hugs and handshakes. He could smell the different kinds of food being prepared in the kitchen. Desmond never ceased to be amazed at how the neighbors would come together to help in a difficult situation. As he walked around the house he had lived in for nineteen years, he reflected on his life growing up and the impact of how well they'd lived with their neighbors. Desmond sat in a chair, leaned back, crossed his arms, and said to the gentleman sitting next to him, "A beautiful life has come to an end."

CHAPTER 6

The day of the funeral came. Desmond was sharply dressed in a black tuxedo. He looked at his mother lying in the casket, her hair well done and affixed with a beautiful rose at the side. It was time for the blue casket to be lowered into the damp earth. It was his mother's express wish to be buried in a blue casket since blue was her favorite color.

Three days after the funeral, Desmond left Greenwood to head back to the military base. He felt the army was the best decision he had yet made. He left Mr. and Mrs. Jones, their closest neighbors and friends of his parents, to look over the family's property. They assured him that all would be well and that he would have nothing to worry about.

Back at the army base, Desmond wanted to get back to life as he'd known it before it had been derailed by the tragic news of his mother's passing. He was a respectable young man. The army defined respect as "something earned, not given." He believed his approach and the way he carried himself and how he treated others would continue to be recognized by his superiors. Desmond understood that respecting people showed where you came from and where you were going. Seeing the best in people gave him motivation and encouragement to become a better soldier.

His superiors' doors were always open if the soldiers needed anything, whether it be professional or personal. Desmond began to build relationships with some of his superior officers. He slowly became part of their loyalty base. He was confident in many situations and didn't seem to be fazed by anyone or anything. He was ambitious and showed the ability to rise through the ranks. His superior officers saw the hunger in him, and they loved what they saw. Desmond was invited by Mr. Todd, the major general of the army, to visit him at his house; the two sat and talked over beers and grilled pork prepared by Mrs. Todd. Desmond was given a tour and was in awe of the beauty of the home. The major said to him, "Young man, you can have this same lifestyle that I am living. You have to pursue what you want, no matter what the consequences might be." Desmond started to adopt his boss's point of view and see the world as his boss saw it.

As time went by, Desmond started to become more antisocial toward his fellow soldiers, lacking empathy and concern for others. He also became manipulative when pitching ideas and would deceive others to get his desired results. Those qualities were exactly what his superiors were looking for in the young soldier. They decided to take him downtown into the city for a night of drinks. He was so excited to be invited out by the big ones. Desmond felt good whenever he was around his superiors. He was well dressed in a white shirt and dark blue jeans. As he sat with crossed legs on a barstool, the handsome young man, who was well proportioned and in great health, gorged himself on a bottle of Johnnie Walker whiskey and spring water. The atmosphere was wonderful, and the music was great; it made him feel relaxed. He said to himself, "I love this place: live music, beautiful setting, and fantastic service, and the food is delicious. I will definitely return." He looked over and saw a couple of women sitting around an oak table, looking as though they were laughing at each other's jokes. He thought he recognized one of the women at the table.

As the conversation continued around him, Desmond could not take his eyes off the woman sitting across from him. He decided to walk over to say hello. He knew his eyes did not deceive him; it was Jade—the woman he'd met when he'd first come to the town. They were both excited to see each other. They talked and exchanged phone numbers. He went back to his table to rejoin his colleagues. The night ended great for him. He went to bed feeling hopeful and happy.

CHAPTER 7

The next morning, Desmond awoke with joy in his heart. The sun rose bright and fair without a cloud to shadow the paths across the sunlit lands. He hurried down the worn stairs. The early-morning sun cast his shadow westward. As he neared, he could hear the sounds of the morning exercise. He started his insane workout. Many aspects of military life were far more difficult than being a civilian. It was disciplined—both physically and mentally tough. Trained and proficient in a warrior's tasks: a guardian of freedom. The training was highly demanding and involved hard physical routine. War offered soldiers raw life: vibrant, terrifying, and full of bliss. It was faced with real danger.

Desmond decided to go out on a limb by asking Jade out on a date. She said yes! They went out on a bush-cooking date. The menu was eddo-leaf callaloo cook-up: rice with roasted fish. It was both of their favorite meals. They gathered some pots, went to the pond, and caught some fish. They made a savory broth of coconut milk with the freshly picked eddo leaf from the fishpond. The catch was a success. He scaled the fish, skinned them, and then put them on sticks and roasted them over the fire. The callaloo was boiling in the coconut milk. You could smell the food from a distance. They sat under a tree that provided cool shade by the edge of the pond. The water was fresh, and they enjoyed each other's company while having the food they'd cooked for lunch. You could tell that love was definitely in the air for them with all the flirting that was happening.

Desmond knew he was falling for Jade. The way he felt about her was like a heartbeat: soft and persistent. Jade laid her head on his lap; as they cuddled, they felt the fresh air on their faces and the wind blowing through their hair. He stared into her brown eyes and pulled her against him as she pressed herself against his heart and comforting chest. He softly kissed her, sweeping his tongue slowly between her lips. She opened her starving mouth, and he sucked on the flesh that was gently swelling inside her mouth. A slight moan escaped from her in response to how he was making her feel. He pulled away for a brief moment, just to look into her eyes. She smiled and slowly started kissing downward toward his chest. He unbuttoned her blouse and slid the bra strap down, softly kissing her shoulder. "Jade," he whispered, then kissed her neck in a way that made her heart dance excitedly. He began kissing her harder, sliding his hand under her breast.

As they got more comfortable on the blanket, he spread her legs and lay on top of her, grinding away on her pussy. He opened his mouth and started sucking on her hot and erect nipples; she growled softly. He slid his fingers on top of hers, together they unzipped his pants. Placing her hands on his erect penis, she began to squeeze it gently. He knew he wanted to be with her for a long time because she was too special to let go, and she was the first woman he had ever kissed. They were both vir-gins and wanted to wait until marriage. They were interrupted by people bringing their cattle home after taking them out in the back fields to graze all day so the cows could get the nourishment to produce milk to sell. Fresh cow's milk was in high demand in the village.

The lovers finished up their afternoon wrapped in each other's arms with kisses on the cheeks and forehead. They headed home full of happiness. A wonderful feeling of excitement filled Desmond as he watched Jade leave.

As the night wrapped up the sky, he lay in bed thinking about her. He couldn't wait to see her again and revisit that anticipation. Something about her was so unique—maybe it was her laughter. "It's so amazing because no one has ever made me laugh as much as she did. Suddenly right there in front of you is everything you need."

As the courtship continued between the handsome soldier and the young schoolteacher, love was definitely in the air for those two lovebirds. *Courtship* was an old-fashioned word used in the Caribbean since the sixteenth century—it meant dating a woman with intentions of marriage and was much more serious than modern dating.

He told Jade while sitting on his couch how much she meant to him and asked her to marry him so they would be no longer two but one flesh. For this reason, a man should leave his mother and father and be joined to his wife to become one. He temporarily moved into his parents' house in order to save money to purchase a new home for them to live in the city, which was closer to the army base. Desmond took his wife around the village to meet the neighbors. Each household wanted her to feel welcome, so they brought baskets to show their appreciation.

As married life began for the Burn's, Desmond and Jade continued their professions as a working family so as to make enough money to move to the big city of lights, where they both could be close to their jobs. He continued to work closely with his superiors, who started to show Desmond how to be desirous of wealth and profits. They shared a scheme to squeeze more money out of people. He was always so ardent about wealth that he wouldn't let his morals get in the way of his pursuit of it. At first, he had been content with his life. Because of the way he was raised by his parents, he was always ambitious and goal oriented, but after stepping out on his own, he become more dissatisfied with the peasant way of his life. After he got into the army, his life became more meaningful, and he began to charge after his goals in an unstoppable way like the speed of a ThrustSSC car. Two years into the military, he was promoted to corporal. He was at the top of his game, performing extremely well under the watchful eyes of his corrupted superiors. Desmond and his commanders would steal smuggled contraband goods from the army's correctional facilities, sell them on the street to local dealers, and split the money among themselves. This was a huge inside circle of corruption, and it was very hard for anyone to detect what was going on.

CHAPTER 8

Jade became pregnant with the couple's first child. Desmond said to Jade, "You are such a special woman, and I can't wait for our baby's arrival."

Jade said to Desmond, "I feel joyful, elated, and empowered to know that in a few months, I will be pushing another human being out of my body. I feel immense gratitude to God above for the ability to conceive. Words can't express it because it feels very fulfilling and satisfying. I like the feeling that there is someone that truly needs me." She continued her teaching job during her pregnancy, but her goal was always to stay safe and comfortable. She was active, upbeat, and cheerful during her pregnancy.

Desmond was excited to share the news with his superiors. He told them he would need to bring in more money because he now had a baby on the way, and he wanted nothing but the best for his family. They explained to him that those deals could only be done at certain times, and if they were not careful, they could be caught. He didn't act too concerned about what they said to him; he was responsible for his decision no matter the ending point, whether it would be success or failure. He didn't want to let his family down.

He called his wife to check in on her. He told his wife, "You are my love. You are my life. You are everything my heart needs. Thank you for saying 'I do' on that special day and making me the happiest man. And I don't ever want you to say that I didn't give you enough because I want my wife to have everything her little heart desires." They were both cheerful people, and their upbeat personalities made it so easy for them to be happy. Happiness was more than a good feeling or a yellow smiley face; it depended on their mindsets and the habits they practiced. It was the "secret sauce" that could help them be and do their best. When people get really good at doing something they enjoy, they can get lost in it. It's called experiencing the best of happiness. Finding ways to use our strengths is a key ingredient for a happy life.

When we are there for the people in our lives and when they're there for us, we are more resilient, resourceful, and successful. We must set realistic goals to turn dreams into realities. The best way to reach any goal is to begin with a specific action. After a while, those actions become habits. That is when those goals can add up to big happiness. But Desmond's pursuit of happiness led him into illegal behavior. His wife began to notice little changes in him, thinking they were caused by a rise in recognition. "He's contributing at a higher level than what his salary was set at since his promotion."

She appreciated the life she was now enjoying. The living situation was now very different from her old apartment. From previous conversations she'd had with her husband, she understood that military life could be a huge barrier to a successful marriage, but she loved her husband and decided to face the music of whatever life threw at her as a military wife. After almost one year of still living in her in-laws' house in the old, dusty village of Greenwood while being pregnant and only able to see her husband every other weekend, it was beginning to feel like a permanent arrangement. The neighbors would check in on Jade to make sure all was well with her and the baby.

To keep her mind occupied while she was pregnant and her husband was away from her, she knitted and sewed, which her mom had taught her how to do at an early age. She also made sure she got everything right, from a healthy diet to good sleep. Jade's mom was of Brazilian descent, and her dad was from Guyana. Brazil and Guyana are neighboring countries. Guyana is bordered by the Atlantic Ocean to the north, by Suriname to the east, by Brazil to the south, and by Venezuela to the west. Both countries were known for their national dishes: Guyana for its mouthwatering cook-up of rice, peas, and meat with vegetables and Brazil for its feijoada—black bean stew. The relationship Jade had with her mom was like no other. They were miles apart and knew that distance could put stress on their relationship. They never let it get between them; they kept their line of communication open as much as they could.

Jade began to get organized before the arrival of her baby. She had lots of furniture and storage space—the changing table and dressing area were supplied with diapers, creams, and wipes. All the bottles, nipples, and pump pieces were sanitized. Every other weekend when Desmond came home, the couple made sure they did a lot of catching up on things.

They welcomed their son, Jack Burns. "I think he is the cutest thing," cried Jade. Motherhood was a wonderful journey for her with many ups and downs. "Every day is a new set of challenges and trials, but I will always be there for my family, and I want them to know that they can count on me, especially this little guy." They announced the arrival of their first baby boy to family and friends. Best wishes and congratulations were sent to the couple in response. Baby gifts from friends, family, and neighbors were delivered to the couple's home, and they were appreciative of all the love they received.

Desmond took some time off to be with his wife and newborn son. He wanted to do everything he could to bond with his son from the start. When bonding with his son, he would place him on his shirtless chest. This was essential and beautiful skin-to-skin contact with his son warm and snug in his arms, Desmond could hear Jack's heartbeat and his breathing. Desmond could feel the bond between him and his son, and it was a beautiful feeling. He wanted them to have a strong father-and-son relationship as Jack grew.

Jade's mom came to stay with her as Desmond was preparing to head back to the army. "No doubt I've enjoyed the comfort of my home and spending quality time with my wife and son, but it's time to head back to work and continue the handling of my business ventures," Desmond thought. A large amount of raw gold had come into the base and had been seized by the army, and he didn't want to miss out on it. He played a role in enforcing the paperwork, and it was one of the army's biggest gold heists. Desmond loved being in the military. It was what he wanted to do, but getting wrapped up with other dirty officers changed him into a different person. He sometimes made the officers uncomfortable; he was that guy that not everybody liked or wanted to work with. The fart from his ass was so tight that even the people in Poland could hear it. He tried to keep his side hustle away from his wife. He told her that due to his promotion, he was able to put more into the household. He knew his wife would not encourage what he was doing, so she couldn't be aware of his actions. He'd known he loved his wife five days after he'd met her. She was also his first sexual experience, so he didn't want anything or anyone to get in the way of his family.

CHAPTER 9

Eight months after the baby was born, Desmond was finally able to purchase a house and move from his parents' old house in Greenwood to his and Jade's brand-new home in the city, which was also closer to his job. This meant his wife and son would get to see him more often. Desmond and Jade decided to ask Jade's mom to come and live with them since they now had a bigger house, so Jade would be able to go back to work and her mom could help raise little Jack. The living arrangement worked out for the Burns family, and everything seemed to be blessed.

The only thing that could bring this family down was Desmond's dark secrets, and he couldn't confess those secrets because it would diminish his ability to live an on-going life, and he wouldn't come clean, not now, not with all the success he had been having.

Jade said to Desmond, "The weekends when you need to stay on the army base and work, I will come up and spend time with you so we can have quality time to ourselves." He was totally fine with the idea his wife had proposed. Respect was necessary for a healthy relationship: it meant that steadfast affection was recognized, supported, and trusted in your relationship and that you valued each other's loyalty and dedication, knowing that you were solely devoted to each other in all the choices and decisions you made.

The army's annual barbecue was coming up. Chefs were invited to compete in a steak contest and four meat divisions of chicken, ribs, pork, and brisket. The steaks were carefully chosen and aged to perfection. The invitation read, "Enjoy the perks of early entry and limited steak samples plus special premium cocktails and samples of wine. A total of $10,000 in prize money will be up for grabs. Over two thousand pounds of mouthwatering certified beef is going to get grilled."

Desmond invited his wife to the army base for the weekend so they could attend the festival. The married couple took part in a sack race and came in first place. This was the first time a collaborative team of husband and wife had won the contest. The trophy depicted a majestic mermaid with a wineglass and a bottle.

The talented six-man army band played beautiful music. The couple enjoyed the tunes, laughing and having a good time with a couple of beers as they hung out with their friends. Desmond introduced his wife to his colleagues. They were a fun group of people, and everyone seemed to be enjoying themselves.

The next morning Desmond took Jade on a run through the trails. A stream ran along the side with several small waterfalls. Gravel and asphalt paths along the route made it very bike friendly. The morning was beautiful, with the wind in their faces considerably more appeal-ing than chugging away on a treadmill. There was a beautiful lake where they could relax and enjoy nature. Decorative wildflowers were growing in the water that made the lake look absolutely beautiful and breathtaking. Desmond and Jade were both passionate about their workouts. They knew that when they worked out together, they motivated each other and cheered each other on. As Jade continued to make frequent trips to visit her husband, she become very familiar with the base, and lots of the soldiers knew who she was. Desmond was selected by the Army

Office Selection Board to train at Sandhurst, England. It was one of the world's most prestigious military institutions. The army had given him a chance offered to very few. The Royal Military Academy Sandhurst was designed to produce well-disciplined soldiers. Training at Sandhurst covered military, practical, and academic subjects. An army career started there: you would begin the special training you needed to be an expert in leadership. Desmond was thrilled that he had been selected by the army for this prestigious achievement.

Training at the Royal Military Academy Sandhurst lasted for forty-four weeks. Term 1 focused on basic military skills: fitness and decision-making. Term 2 continued the development of leadership skills and had a major academic component. Term 3 put the officers' skills into practice. Desmond, being an international soldier, built lifelong friendships and connections while training at Sandhurst. His best friend was a British soldier who was a lawyer and intelligence officer. The two soldiers gave themselves the nickname "Steel Horses." They pushed themselves to learn how much they could do and how much they couldn't. They would push their sweat-soaked bodies hard to master their skills, which took hard work, intense training, and dedication. Both soldiers graduated from Sandhurst as second lieutenants.

On the last day of training, the men were looking forward to going home. Desmond said to his friend "I am looking forward to the privilege of seeing my country when I return." Desmond returned to his native country, Guyana. The prime minister paid tribute to him, and he was promoted to sergeant for completing his training at Sandhurst in Bracknell Forest. He had set an example not only for his colleagues but for all officers at Royal Academic Military Sandhurst. "Thank you for your service to this country; your bravery, sacrifice, and strength will not go unnoticed. We owe so much to you and your family, and you are what makes this country a better place."

Desmond was full of egotism. He was arrogant, cocky, overconfident, and selfish, generally thinking he was better than other people. He was suffering from an inflated ego, he was never satisfied with what he got, he always wanted more, he was perceived to be full of his own importance by Mr. Todd, and he was addicted to the high he got from reaching goals. The overvaluation of his ego made him appear childish. He was absorbed in his own grandiosity. Some of his superiors started to worry about him—that if he allowed his ego to get unchecked, it could cause tremendous turmoil not only for him but for them as well. But because of his value to their gold-smuggling ring, they would frequently go to great lengths to work with him.

CHAPTER 10

The key to success was not having to deal with a team member making a situation difficult. Thinking Desmond's behavior would change since he'd just gotten back from a prestigious academy as an effective leader, his superiors decided to have a talk with him because getting to the bottom of the situation without alienating him was essential. So they confronted him with a productive approach about his egotistical behavior. Some progress was made toward improving his attitude, which was like a flat tire: you cannot go anywhere until you change it. After the meeting, Desmond started to shift his mindset because he realized it played a major role in both motivation and achievement. His appearance of modeling good behavior was all fake. The drawback of this approach was that it could require significant effort, but he played it all cool so that they would continue to trust him to handle all the illegal paperwork so he could keep filling his pocket with racketeering money. They used the land-based military branch as a smuggling base instead of a military branch that served its country in times of war and peace.

One evening Desmond came home very early. He walked through the old gate at the back of the yard that led to a shed where he stored his garden tools. He sat on the bench that was braced against the wall of the shed. In his hands was a brown leather bag. Dusk fell, but Jade still recognized the color of the bag he was carrying. He planted the bag in the shed as she watched him from the back kitchen window. He came into the house and was bombarded with questions from Jade about what he was hiding in the shed. He revealed to Jade that he and some friends had invested time, energy, and cash into a new project that would take time away from work, so he hid some money in the shed so that they could use it to buy material for the project. He didn't want the money in the house, so he'd left it there to be separate from everything else. He stood by the door of the brick house as he continued to explain his actions.

The next evening on his way home from work, Desmond drove past his house. He wanted to minimize any hassle from his wife, so he stopped at the local tavern for a drink. He ordered a Guinness and sat in the corner of the room. After finishing the bottle, he returned to the bartender and ordered two more bottles. The bar also served pizza, burgers, and fries. As he continued to sit with his beer, he watched as the place of business entertained people gathered for food and drink. The location near the boardwalk and beach was a plus for the tavern. It was a very good night for the pub as more people came in to have fun.

Desmond left the bar, got into his car, pulled away from the curb, and headed home. The house was so quiet you could hear a pin drop. The nursery was quiet; everyone had gone to sleep, so Desmond decided to surf the internet, read, and watch television. It felt like a bit of freedom not having to deal with Jade and the arguments that had started when he hid the brown leather bag in the shed. He poured himself a glass of wine and turned the music on very low. Wine and music had always been a perfect pair. Listening to the mellow, soft, and subtle music, he went into the gallery, sat on a lounge chair, and gazed at the moonlit sky, trying to identify the planets. Zach, an old friend of Desmond, called to tell him about the sex club that he'd visited after his shift at the bar, but

Desmond hardly listened. Zach was still young at heart, while Desmond was a married man with responsibilities.

Desmond didn't feel connected with his wife. He'd lost interest in their physical intimacy; his mind was focused on making money, so he'd put their physical connection on the back burner. Jade revealed to Desmond that she wanted to try to do things to bulletproof their marriage, such as having date nights and getting into bed together to add structure to their relationship. While helping foster intimacy, the bedroom can seem to contain the heart of a marriage. This was the routine Jade wanted to have when Desmond was home on the weekends and off from work.

As he sat on the lounge chair, he took the last sips of his wine and placed the glass on a coaster on the smooth mahogany desk. He decided to sleep on the couch instead of the bed due to the fight he'd had with his wife the night before. He might just sleep better without someone stealing the sheets and involuntarily kicking him throughout the night.

CHAPTER 11

Early the next morning, Jade woke up around 4:30 a.m. to run her usual five miles. Desmond was still asleep on the couch. Jade loved to do her solo morning jog through the woods. It was quiet and peaceful, and it was her time for herself before she took care of anyone else. She was trying to lose weight by running before eating breakfast, which helped increased her metabolism and burned more calories.

Desmond got up and took a shower, which helped put him in a good mood and relaxed him. He started the morning off with a healthy breakfast of oatmeal, nuts, eggs, fruit, and pudding. He would boost his energy level and break the fast he'd put his body through while sleeping. In the meantime, Jade got back from her run. Desmond asked her to join him for breakfast. She got cleaned up and joined her husband on the terrace overlooking their beautiful garden that her mother had created—it looked kind of like Napa Valley, the perfect oasis for relaxation and romance. Desmond and Jade discussed the unproductive conflict between them during their argument. They promised each other to have more productive conflict, hearing each other's thoughts and feelings without criticism. Disagreements didn't need to end in hostile silence. Marriage was hard to maintain, and it was possible for couples to fall out of love with each other. It was also difficult to maintain the level of excitement felt between a man and a woman when they first met once they were sharing their lives together. Marital satisfaction decreased sharply when kids became part of the relationship. Desmond needed to have foreplay with his wife. He missed the way she used to go down on his penis, but since the baby came along, she refused, saying her mouth was what she kissed their son with. Desmond thought it was up to his wife and how willing she was to participate in their marriage.

The seizing of contraband took a hit because smugglers were being more careful of the army and police. They were tired of having their goods seized by the military, so they decided to take different approaches to keep their contraband out of the army's and police's hands. Desmond started to feel a sense of stagnation; things weren't happening the way they were supposed to.

Desmond decided to have Jade come to the base while he was there for the weekend. When she got there, he was gone for the day to do training exercises. She started to snoop around, trying to find out if any of her husband's friends knew anything about his business venture. She walked over to Tom's room, trying to see what she could find out. Tom and Desmond had been friends since they'd joined the army together. Tom was very laid back and kept to himself most of the time, and Desmond loved that about him. She told him about the leather bag that her husband had brought home and hid in the shed in the backyard. Tom responded, "I don't know anything, and why don't you talk to your husband instead of talking to me? This ain't no time for you to be snooping around. As many people know, snooping on your partner is never a good idea."

As she started walking back to her room, she could see the sun starting to duck behind the clouds. She glanced at her watch, and it was four o'clock in the afternoon. Desmond returned to base after being out all day. He always tried to create a lasting routine with his training. Desmond took Jade across to the officer's club for a drink. He did not have to wear his uniform while drinking at the bar. He led the way to the bar and passed some tables where soldiers sat drinking and others were playing poker. He leaned over and whispered into Jade's ear, "My intent is to never drink at a bar with these guys but rather have a meal in the restaurant. They will stay at the bar until they have consumed enough booze." He pulled her close and grinned wickedly.

She said to him, "You're funny," and gave a slight shrug of her shoulders.

The grand wooden army bar was made out of polished greenheart wood. It was a bar and a restaurant specializing in cocktails and seasonal vegetable dishes. After dinner they joined the secretary of defense, with whom they engaged in conversation. A young woman walked up to them and said, "Hey, Desmond."

"Ooh, wow, I think I am seeing a ghost—I can't believe it's you!" Desmond exclaimed. It was his cousin whom he hadn't seen in years. Desmond had always had a problem with the guy she was dating, which was why they stayed out of touch with one another, but his cousin reminded him that she had been dating this guy for years and the journey had been great.

"The most important thing is that he loves me unconditionally. We are happy together; he proposed to me, so I think you should stop focusing on how much you hate him and try to get to know him."

The two women were introduced after Desmond had to get his feelings across the table about his cousin's relationship. Jade asked her husband, "Why don't you like the guy?"

Desmond summed it up in three words: "He's an asshole."

Tom, his friend, walked into the bar. Jade was a bit nervous. She didn't know if he would say anything to her husband about her visit to him. Desmond gave him a high five.

She said hello, and he went on to order his drink.

CHAPTER 12

The next day Desmond found out his wife had been snooping around, asking questions about his business. Word started to spread, and Desmond was summoned by his superiors, who told him he had to keep his wife on a leash or she could destroy things for the union. That made Desmond very angry. He spoke to his wife about what he had found out. They got into a very heated argument about trust issues in their marriage. Desmond was so pissed off at Jade that he walked over to the living room couch where she was laying, grabbed her by her hands, and pressed her hard against the cushions. He started screaming at her, "Stay out of my fucking business! It's none of yours what I do. Stop snooping around. What you don't know will not hurt you." She got up, poured herself a glass of wine, and stared out the window, tears streaming down her cheeks. She started packing her stuff and left the base for home, contemplating divorce, even though it was the first time he'd laid his hands on her. She was not going to let him do it again. The officers asked him if he had the situation under control. He told them he had gently tugged on the leash, so she would stop.

Jade arrived home and called Desmond to tell him to find somewhere else to live and that she was filing for divorce and would report him to the army captain. She had had enough of his abuse. She used threatening words with him, so he complied with her terms. He told her he would go to his friend Tom's apartment when he was off the base on weekends. The friends split the two-bedroom, one-bathroom apartment.

The couple was separated for four months. He would come by as much as he could to visit his son so they could have some father-and-son time. He loved his son very much. Chances were that the relationship between mother and son would come before Desmond's relationship with Jack, but when Desmond visited his son, he would hold, hug, and cuddle with him as much as he could. He would talk to his friends about the situation, and they would advise him to let Jade calm down and then try to talk to her. Desmond would respond, "I am trying to be civil for our child, but she keeps shutting me out every time I try to talk to her. I don't know how long it'll last."

In the meantime, Jade was getting tired of Desmond's emotional mind-fucking games. "I just want everything to stop and to raise my son alone." She told him to take care of their son financially—be a father to him, and she would do the rest—but Desmond said he'd changed and was ready to come home. Still, there was no sign of reconciliation.

Desmond thought to himself "how do I convince my separated wife to give me a second chance? I don't want to lose my wife forever." One evening he called Jade over the phone. "I have been trying my hardest to get you back into my life. I know you don't want to get back together with me, but can we at least be friends from now on and also be civil and do what is best for our son?"

She was quiet on the other end of the phone, listening to him pleading his case. For a little bit, she felt a sudden thunder of pity for him. She was worried about him, and she was touched by the idea that she felt pity for him, but little did she know that she was in more danger than she realized.

Desmond knew in his heart that he would never let Jade go. He was feeling like someone was ripping his heart from his chest. He knew he had to fight hard. He knew that she knew too much about the illegal dealing that went on in the army, and if she opened her mouth, they could all go to jail for a really long time, so he knew he had to get her back and work things out with her. Desmond started using manipulative tactics. He began by giving her space and making sure his son's needs were met, which was his obligation. He even started going back to church on a regular basis. The last time he did such was when his parents were alive. After a while, even his friends noticed the changes in him. Some of them even suggested to Jade that maybe it was time to talk to him and see how things went, so she decided to give in and give him a chance.

She tried to tolerate him. He thanked her for talking to him and asked her if she would consider going out to dinner and talking more. Jade told her friends about Desmond's suggestions. They told her to give him a chance. "You may say he is not ideal; he is not perfect. He is not Prince Charming straight out of a fairy tale. Loving relationships have always been one of the most important and complicated things in life. They can either bring joy and positivity or fill life with resentment and sorrow. Just trust your heart and your feelings."

CHAPTER 13

It was Friday; the weekend was almost here. Jade called Desmond and told him she was ready to talk. She wanted to meet up for dinner, but he told her he was on the army base for the weekend and that they were throwing a surprise party for a senior officer. He said she should come up and bring some nice clothing so they could attend the party; plus, there would be lot of privacy. Perhaps she could bring her running gear to go for the early-morning run that she loved.

She packed up and headed to the army base, where she would have the long-awaited talk with her husband. Desmond picked up a magazine that was sitting on the coffee table, pretending to read it. He decided to hatch a devious plan against his wife. He would not let her stand in his way, so he decided to murder her. All he needed was a piece of nylon rope. Desmond and Jade attended the surprise party; she was dressed in a beautiful red evening gown that amplified her femininity. He wore a light blue suit that accentuated his dark skin. He was masculine and dignified in his attire, and Jade's long black hair fell in curls over her shoulders. He led her to the balcony overlooking the barrack square where drills were performed. The makeup reflected light that gave her skin a luminous glow, and she looked like the epitome of elegance and good taste.

Once they returned to the room, Desmond slept on the couch while Jade slept on the bed. He wanted to make sure she was comfortable around him and that she could trust him, and he did everything to make sure his trust was earned. Desmond was charismatic, and everybody knew it. He knew what to do to make people entrust themselves to him.

Jade woke up early to a view of the sunrise and a cold, frosty morning. She could hardly see a thing outside as she and Desmond prepared to go for a run down their favorite trails that they both loved so much. As they began running, you could see warm moisture from their breath caused by the cold air. They ran for about fifteen minutes; little did she know she was running to her grave.

He wanted her to get a little tired so the chance of her defending herself wouldn't be a factor. Desmond came to a sudden stop. She asked him if he was okay. He walked toward her with a sad look on his face. They heard noises; it was some other soldiers getting their morning exercise on the other side of the trail. He grabbed her and started kissing her passionately and pressing his hands to her crotch. She tried to resist, but the passion was too strong for her. She started to get weak in the knees. He laid her down on the soft, wet grass, grinding on her vagina as he slipped his hand into her panties and used his fingers to penetrate her pussy, which was very wet. He knew she wanted him; he began to get rough with her, biting her tits.

He ripped her pants off and rolled her on her stomach. She began moaning and groaning as he slid his dick up her wet pussy and began penetrating her really hard from behind. He took the nylon rope and tied her hands behind her back; she now was helpless. He pulled his dick out of her pussy and used another piece of rope to strangle her until she was unconscious. He then dragged her lifeless body through the wet grass until he came upon a manhole. He placed her neck over the rim of the manhole and stomped on her neck as hard as he could until it was broken.

Then he placed her head into the manhole, leaving her body out. He used his feet to push the upper and then lower part of the body down as far as he could, leaving just her feet out. He placed the cover of the manhole on her feet. He wanted to make sure the scent of the decomposition of the body would make it easy for her to be discovered. He fled the scene and went back to the base and continued his normal routine.

CHAPTER 14

When Jade never made it home that Sunday morning, her mom called Desmond's phone to speak with her. He told her mother that she was not with him and that he'd put her on a bus back home. Her mother stated that she had never come home. Her mom was very worried and started to call her friends and ask if they had seen her, but everyone's response was no. Desmond went to his superiors to let them know that his wife was nowhere to be found and he needed to go home to see what was going on. He needed some leave of absence. Desmond called the police to report that his wife was missing. Because of his status as an army officer, immediate action was taken, and the search began to find the officer's missing wife. The news began hitting the airwaves with a request to anyone who knew anything or had heard anything to please come forward; their identity would remain anonymous. This went on for two weeks, but no one came forward. Flyers with her picture were placed on every light post, on trees, and on fences. Desmond was very cooperative with the authorities in trying to locate his missing wife. One early morning back at the army base, two soldiers were walking the trails when they came up upon a foul odor. They followed the scent to a narrow grassy knoll about one hundred yards outside the army's property. They stumbled upon a body in the grave of a manhole. The men reported it to the army, who then called the police.

The woman's body was identified as that of Jade Burns. Officers went to the home of Desmond Burn's and placed him under arrest for the murder of his wife, but Desmond maintained his innocence. Jade's mom watched as her son-in-law was led away in handcuffs for the murder of her daughter while her grandson slept peacefully on the bed. Jade's mom revealed to neighbors that her heart was heavy with grief. "I miss her so much. I lost my beautiful, caring, funny, intelligent daughter, who fell victim to nothing but pure evil." But friends and relatives of Desmond Burns stood behind him to show their support for the disgraced officer.

Desmond sought legal help from a friend he'd met at the academy when he was in training. The friend was a lawyer and an army officer who was on a special assignment in South America. For both army officers and lawyers, leadership skills were essential. This man took a special interest in the case of his friend and joined his legal defense team, the lawyers based their case on "no eyewitness".

As the prosecution and defense teams rested their cases and the jury began their deliberation, the city of Georgetown was on high alert. The story had captivated the nation. The city was on verdict watch. The jury deliberated for two days and reached a verdict. The courtroom was packed; the streets were crowded. Police officers and army officers were on standby. Those who weren't able to get close to the courthouse listened on the radio and watched on television. It was one thirty in the afternoon when the verdict was read. The city was preparing for bloodshed between the Burns family and Jade's family. The military was on alert to keep the peace.

At 1:30 p.m., court was back in session. The foreman stood up. "We find the defendant, Desmond Burns, not guilty." It was pandemonium in the city of Georgetown. The courtroom where the verdict had been announced was in a wild uproar with an eruption of anger and excitement.

Desmond was quickly whisked away from the courtroom by the army, down the stairs, and through a tunnel under the courthouse, where an army vehicle was waiting for the lieutenant officer who had just been given another chance at life. The judge and jury were all taken away to a safe and secluded area.

Violence began to erupt in the streets, and angry mobs started to throw bottles and rocks into the crowd. People were running for their lives helter-skelter away from the confusion. There were cries and shouts from the main gate; you could see huge flames and black smoke.

Desmond was taken to the safe house of a trusted family member to take refuge. He was given every manner of protection possible. Desmond still continued to receive his salary from the army. While he was in the safe hiding place, he was able to save a lot of money. He wanted to leave the country and start a new life.

Jade's mom was given full custody of her grandson, and Desmond was not allowed to go to the house he'd once shared with his wife and young son. Jade's cousins wanted to take the love they'd had for her out on the body of the man who'd killed her. There was bad blood between the two families after the murder and the acquittal. The two warring families built up a lot of anger and hostility. Desmond wanted to burn the Santiagos' house down while they were asleep in it and put an end to the family. But he was told it did no good to get upset over a bad decision during an unfortunate situation that had already passed. Desmond was a trained soldier from the Academy Sandhurst who had special skills and knew how to use them well. He was warned not to drain more blood out of the family. A great deal of blood had already been spilled.

After two years of hiding out in the safe house, Desmond got the break he needed: he got a visa for London. He sat in the back of his cousin's car on the way to the airport.

His flight was at five o'clock that morning. Things were so tense between the families that there was no telling who would see him and recognize him. He'd disguised himself by growing a beard and wearing a baseball cap. But he got safely to the airport. It wasn't safe for him to live in the country anymore; he was scared and couldn't have a normal life since Jade's family wanted him dead. He bid his cousin farewell and left the shores of Guyana.